NICOLAS FLAMEL AND THE PHILOSOPHER'S STONE

The name of this alchemical adept has been profoundly venerated not only in the memory of the Hermetists but in the hearts of the French people, among whom he is the central figure of many marvellous legends and traditions. "Whilst in all ages and nations the majority of hierophants have derived little but deception, ruination, and despair as the result of their devotion to alchemy, Nicholas Flamel enjoyed permanent good fortune and serenity. Far from expending his resources in the practice of the *magnum opus*, he added with singular suddenness a vast treasure to a moderate fortune. These he employed in charitable endowments and in pious foundations that long survived him and long sanctified his memory. He built churches and chapels which were adorned with statues of himself, accompanied by symbolical characters and mysterious crosses, which subsequent adepts long strove to decipher, that they might discover his secret history, and the kabbalistic description of the process by which he was conducted to the realisation of the Grand Magisterium."

Whether Flamel was born at Paris or Pontoise is not more uncertain than the precise date of his nativity. This occurred some time during the reign of Philippe le Bel, the spoliator of the grand order of the Temple, and, on the whole, the most probable year is 1330. His parents were poor, and left him little more than the humble house in Paris which he continued to possess till his death, and which he eventually bequeathed to the Church. It stood in Notary Street, at the corner of Marivaux Street, opposite the Marivaux door of the Church of Saint-Jacques-la-Boucherie.

Authorities disagree as to the amount of education that

Flamel obtained in his youth, but it was sufficient to qualify him for the business of a scrivener, which, in spite of his wealth and his accredited wisdom, he continued to follow through life. He was proficient in painting and poetry, and had a taste for architecture and the mathematical sciences ; yet he applied himself steadily to business, and contracted a prudent marriage, his choice falling on a widow, named Pernelle, who, though handsome, was over forty years, but who brought a considerable dowry to her second husband.

In his capacity as a copyist before the age of printing, books of all classes fell into the hands of Flamel, and among them were many of those illuminated alchemical treatises which are reckoned among the rarest treasures of mediæval manuscripts. Acquainted with the Latin language, he insensibly accumulated an exotéric knowledge of the aims and theories of the adepts. His interest and curiosity were awakened, and he began studying them in his leisure moments. Now tradition informs us that, whether his application was great, his desire intense, or whether he was super-eminently fitted to be included by divine election among the illuminated Sons of the Doctrine, or for whatever other reason, the mystical Bath-Kôl appeared to him under the figure of an angel, bearing a remarkable book bound in well-wrought copper, the leaves of thin bark, graven right carefully with a pen of iron. An inscription in characters of gold contained a dedication addressed to the Jewish nation by Abraham the Jew, prince, priest, astrologer, and philosopher.

" Flamel," cried the radiant apparition, " behold this book of which thou understandest nothing ; to many others but thyself it would remain for ever unintelligible, but one day thou shalt discern in its pages what none but thyself will see !"

At these words Flamel eagerly stretched out his hands to take possession of the priceless gift, but book and angel disappeared in an auriferous tide of light. The scrivener awoke to be ravished henceforth by the divine dream of alchemy; but so long a time passed without any fulfilment of the angelic promise, that the ardour of his imagination cooled, the great hope dwindled gradually away, and he was settling once more into the commonplace existence of a plodding scribe, when, on a certain day of election in the year 1357, an event occurred which bore evidence of the veracity of his visionary promise-maker, and exalted his ambition and aspirations to a furnace heat. This event, with the consequences it entailed, are narrated in the last testament of Nicholas Flamel, which begins in the following impressive manner, but omits all reference to the legendary vision :—

" The Lord God of my life, who exalts the humble in spirit out of the most abject dust, and makes the hearts of such as hope in Him to rejoice, be eternally praised.

" Who, of His own grace, reveals to the believing souls the springs of His bounty, and subjugates beneath their feet the crowns of all earthly felicities and glories.

" In Him let us always put our confidence, in His fear let us place our happiness, and in His mercy the hope and glory of restoration from our fallen state.

" And in our supplications to Him let us demonstrate or show forth a faith unfeigned and stable, an assurance that shall not for ever be shaken.

"·And Thou, O Lord God Almighty, as Thou, out of Thy infinite and most desirable goodness, hast condescended to open the earth and unlock Thy treasures unto me, Thy poor and unworthy servant, and hast given into my possession the fountains and well-springs of all the treasures and riches of this world.

"So, O Lord God, out of Thine abundant kindness, extend Thy mercies unto me, that when I shall cease to be any longer in the land of the living, Thou mayst open unto me the celestial riches, the divine treasures, and give me a part or portion in the heavenly inheritance for ever.

"Where I may behold Thy divine glory and the fulness of Thy Heavenly Majesty, a pleasure, so ineffable, and a joy, so ravishing, which no mortal can express or conceive.

"This I entreat of Thee, O Lord, for our Lord Jesus Christ, Thy well-beloved Son's sake, who in the unity of the Holy Spirit liveth with Thee, world without end. Amen.

"I, *Nicholas Flamel*, Scrivener, living at *Paris*, anno 1399, in the *Notary Street*, near *St James*, of the *Bouchery*, though I learned not much Latin, because of the poorness and meanness of my parents, who were notwithstanding (by them that envy me most) accounted honest and good people.

"Yet, by the blessing of God, I have not wanted an understanding of the books of the philosophers, but learned them and attained to a certain kind of knowledge, even of their hidden secrets.

"For which cause sake there shall not any moment of my life pass, wherein remembering this so vast a good, I will not on my bare knees, if the place will permit of it, or otherwise in my heart, with all the entireness of my affections, render thanks to this my most good and precious God.

"Who never forsakes the righteous generation, or suffers the children of the just to beg their bread, nor deceives their expectations, but supports them with blessings who put their trust in Him.

"After the death of my parents, I, *Nicholas Flamel*, got

my living by the art of writing, engrossing inventories, making up accounts, keeping of books, and the like.

"In this course of living there fell by chance into my hands a gilded book, very old and large, which cost me only two *florins*.

"It was not made of paper or parchment, as other books are, but of admirable rinds (as it seemed to me) of young trees. The cover of it was of *brass;* it was well bound, and graven all over with a strange kind of letters, which I take to be Greek characters, or some such like.

"This I know that I could not read them, nor were they either Latin or French letters, of which I understand something.

"But as to the matter which was written within, it was engraven (as I suppose) with an iron pencil or graver upon the said bark leaves, done admirably well, and in fair and neat Latin letters, and curiously coloured.

"It contained thrice seven leaves, for so they were numbered in the top of each folio, and every seventh leaf was without any writing, but in place thereof there were several images or figures painted.

"Upon the first seventh leaf was depicted—1. A Virgin. 2. Serpents swallowing her up. On the second seventh, a serpent crucified; and on the last seventh, a desert or wilderness, in midst whereof were seen many fair fountains, whence issued out a number of serpents here and there.

"Upon the first of the leaves was written in capital letters of gold, Abraham the Jew, Priest, Prince, Levite, Astrologer, and Philosopher, to the nation of the Jews dispersed by the wrath of God in France, wisheth health.

"After which words, it was filled with many execrations and curses, with this word MARANATHA, which was oft repeated against any one that should look in to unfold it, except he were either Priest or Scribe.

" The person that sold me this book was ignorant of its worth as well as I who bought it. I judge it might have been stolen from some of the Jewish nation, or else found in some place where they anciently abode.

" In the second leaf of the book he consoled his nation, and gave them pious counsel to turn from their wickedness and evil ways, but above all to flee from idolatry, and to wait in patience for the coming of the Messiah, who, conquering all the kings and potentates of the earth, should reign in glory with his people to eternity. Without doubt, this was a very pious, wise, and understanding man.

" In the third leaf, and in all the writings that followed, he taught them, in plain words, the transmutation of metals, to the end that he might help and assist his dispersed people to pay their tribute to the Roman Emperors, and some other things not needful here to be repeated.

" He painted the vessels by the side or margin of the leaves, and discovered all the colours as they should arise or appear, with all the rest of the work.

" But of the *prima materia* or first matter, or agent, he spake not so much as one word ; but only he told them that in the fourth and fifth leaves he had entirely painted or decyphered it, and depicted or figured it, with a desirable dexterity and workmanship.

" Now though it was singularly well and materially or intelligibly figured and painted, yet by that could no man ever have been able to understand it without having been well skilled in their Cabala, which is a series of old traditions, and also to have been well studied in their books.

" The fourth and fifth leaf thereof was without any writing, but full of fair figures, bright and shining, or, as it were, enlightened, and very exquisitely depicted.

"First, there was a young man painted, with wings at his ankles, having in his hand a caducean rod, writhen about with two serpents, wherewith he stroke upon an helmet covering his head.

"This seemed in my mean apprehension to be one of the heathen gods, namely, Mercury. Against him there came running and flying with open wings, a great old man with an hour-glass fixed upon his head, and a scythe in his hands, like Death, with which he would (as it were in indignation) have cut off the feet of Mercury.

"On the other side of the fourth leaf he painted a fair flower, on the top of a very high mountain, which was very much shaken by the north wind. Its footstalk was blue, its flowers white and red, and its leaves shining like fine gold, and round about it the dragons and griffins of the north made their nests and habitations.

"On the fifth leaf was a fair rose-tree, flowered, in the midst of a garden, growing up against a hollow oak, at the foot whereof bubbled forth a fountain of pure white water, which ran headlong down into the depths below.

"Yet it passed through the hands of a great number of people who digged in the earth, seeking after it, but, by reason of their blindness, none of them knew it, except a very few, who considered its weight.

"On the last side of the leaf was depicted a king, with a faulchion, who caused his soldiers to slay before him many infants, the mothers standing by, and weeping at the feet of their murderers.

"These infants' blood being gathered up by other soldiers, was put into a great vessel wherein Sol and Luna came to bathe themselves.

"And because this history seemed to represent the destruction of the Innocents by Herod, and that I learned the chiefest part of the art in this book, therefore I placed in their churchyard these hieroglyphic figures of this learning. Thus have you that which was contained in the first five leaves.

"As for what was in all the rest of the written leaves, which was wrote in good and intelligible Latin, I must conceal, lest God being offended with me should send His plague and judgments upon me. It would be a wickedness much greater than he who wished that all men in the world had but one head, that he might cut it off at a blow.

"Having thus obtained this delicate and precious book, I did nothing else day and night but study it; conceiving very well all the operations it pointed forth, but wholly ignorant of the *prima materia* with which I should begin, which made me very sad and discontented.

"My wife, whose name was Perrenelle, whom I loved equally with myself, and whom I had but lately married, was mightily concerned for me, and, with many comforting words, earnestly desired to know how she might deliver me from this trouble.

"I could no longer keep counsel, but told her all, shewing her the very book, which, when she saw, she became as well pleased with it as myself, and with great delight beheld the admirable cover, the engraving, the images, and exquisite figures thereof, but understood them as little as I.

"Yet it was matter of consolation to me to discourse and entertain myself with her, and to think what we should do to find out the interpretation and meaning thereof.

"At length I caused to be painted within my chamber, as much to the life or original as I could, all the images and figures of the said fourth and fifth leaves.

"These I showed to the greatest scholars and most learned men in Paris, who understood thereof no more than myself: I told them they were found in a book which taught the philosophers' stone.

" But the greatest part of them made a mock both of me and that most excellent secret, except one whose name was Anselm, a practiser of physic and a deep student in this art.

" He much desired to see my book, which he valued more than anything else in the world, but I always refused him, only making him a large demonstration of the method.

" He told me that the first figure represented Time, which devours all things, and that, according to the number of the six written leaves, there was required a space of six years to perfect the stone; and then, said he, we must turn the glass and see it no more.

" I told him this was not painted, but only to show the teacher the *prima materia*, or first agent, as was written in the book. He answered me that this digestion for six years was, as it were, a second agent, and that certainly the first agent was there painted, which was a white and heavy water.

" This, without doubt, was *argent vive*, which they could not fix ; that is, cut off his feet, or take away his volubility, save by that long digestion in the pure blood of young infants.

" For in that this *argent vive* being joined with Sol and Luna was first turned with them into a plant, like that there painted, and afterwards by corruption into serpents, which serpents, being perfectly dried and digested, were made a fine powder of gold, which is the stone.

" This strange or foreign discourse to the matter was the cause of my erring, and that made me wander for the space of one and twenty years in a perfect meander from the verity; in which space of time I went through a thousand labyrinths or processes, but all in vain; yet never with the blood of infants, for that I accounted wicked and villainous.

"For I found in my book that the philosophers called blood the mineral spirit which is in the metals, chiefly in Sol, Luna, and Mercury, to which sense I always, in my own judgment, assented. Yet these interpretations were, for the most part, not more subtle than true.

"Not finding, therefore, in my operation or course of the process, the signs, at the time written in my book, I was ever to begin again.

"In the end, having lost all hope of ever understanding those symbols or figures, I made a vow to God to demand their interpretation of some Jewish priest belonging to some synagogue in Spain.

"Whereupon, with the consent of my wife Perrenelle, carrying with me the extract or copy of the figures or pictures, I took up a pilgrim's habit and staff, in the same manner as you see me figured without the said arch, in the said churchyard in which I put these Hieroglyphic Figures.

"Whereupon also I have set on the wall, on both hands, the process, representing in order all the colours of the stone, as they rise and go away again.

"This is, as it were, the very beginning of Hercules his book, entitled 'Iris, or the Rainbow,' which treats of the stone in these words:—*The process of the work is very pleasing unto nature.*

"And these words I also put there expressly, for the sake of great scholars and learned men, who may understand to what they allude.

"In this same manner, I say, I put myself upon my journey to Spain, and so much I did that I, in a short time, arrived at Mountjoy, and, a while after, at St James, where, with much devotion, I accomplished my vow.

"This done, in Leon, I, at my return, met with a merchant of Boulogne, who brought me acquainted with a physician, M. Canches, a Jew by nation, but now a Christian, dwelling at Leon aforesaid.

"I showed him the extract or copy of my figures, by which he was, as it were, ravished with great astonishment and joy. He desired immediately if I could tell him any news of the book whence they were drawn.

"I answered him in Latin (in which language he asked me the question) that I doubted not of obtaining the sight of the book, if I could meet with any one who could unfold the enigmas. Hearing this, and being transported with great earnestness and joy, he began to decypher unto me the beginning.. To be short, he was much pleased that he was in hopes to hear tidings of the book, and I as much pleased to hear him speak and interpret it. And, doubtless, he had heard much talk of the book, but it was, as he said, of a thing which was believed to be utterly lost. Upon this, we resolved for our voyage, and from Leon we passed to Oviedo, and thence to Sareson, where we took shipping, and went to sea in order to go into France.

"Our voyage was prosperous and happy, and, being arrived in the kingdom of France, he most truly interpreted unto me the greatest part of my figures, in which, even to the points and pricks, he could decypher great mysteries, which were admirable to me. Having attained Orleans, this learned man fell sick, even to death, being afflicted with extreme vomitings, which still continued with him, as being first caused by sea-sickness. Notwithstanding which, he was in continual fear lest I should leave or forsake him, which was a great trouble to him. And although I was continually by his side, yet he would be almost always calling for me. At the end of the seventh day of his sickness he died, which was no small grief to me, and I buried him, as well as my condition would permit me, in a church at Orleans.

"He that would see the manner of my arrival and the joy of Perrenelle, let him look upon us two in the city of Paris, upon the door of the chapel of James of the Boucherie, close by the one side of my house, where we are both painted, kneeling and giving thanks to God. For through the grace of God it was that I attained the perfect knowledge of all I desired.

"Well, I had now the *prima materia*, the first principles, yet not their first preparation, which is a thing most difficult above all other things in the world; but in the end I had that also, after a long aberration, and wandering in a labyrinth of errors for the space of three years, or thereabouts, during which time I did nothing but study and search and labour, so as you see me depicted without this arch where I have placed my process; praying also continually unto God, and reading attentively in my book, pondering the words of the philosophers, and then trying and proving the various operations, which I thought to myself they might mean by their words. At length I found that which I desired, which I also soon knew by the scent and odour thereof. Having this, I easily accomplished the magistery. For knowing the preparations of the prime agents, and then literally following the directions in my book, I could not then miss the work if I would.

"Having attained this, I come now to projection; the first time I made projection was upon mercury, a pound and a half whereof, or thereabouts, I turned into pure silver, better than that of the mine, as I proved by assaying of it myself, and also causing others to assay it for me several times. This was done in the year of our Lord 1382, January 17, about noon, being Monday, in my own house, Perrenelle only present.

"Again, following exactly the directions in my book, literally and word by word, I made projection of the red stone, on the like quantity, Perrenelle only being present, and in the same house, which was done in the same year of our Lord, namely, 1382, April 25, at five in the afternoon. This mercury I truly transmuted into almost as much gold, much better, indeed, than common gold, more soft also, and more pliable.

"I speak it in all truth: I have made it three times, with the help of Perrenelle, who understood it as well as myself, because she assisted me in my operations. And without doubt, if she would have done it alone, she would have brought it to the same, or full as great, perfection as I had done. I had truly enough when I had once done it: but I found exceeding great pleasure and delight in seeing and contemplating *the admirable works of Nature within the vessels*, and to show to you that I had thus done it three times, I caused to be depicted under the same arch, three furnaces, like to those which serve for the operations of this work.

"I was much concerned for a long time lest Perrenelle, by reason of extreme joy, should not hide her felicity, which I measured by my own, and lest she should let fall some words among her relations concerning the great treasure we possessed. For an extremity of joy takes away the understanding as well as an extremity of grief and sorrow. But the goodness of the most great God had not only given and filled me with this blessing, to give me a chaste and sober wife, but she was also a wise and prudent woman, not only capable of reason but also to do what was reasonable, and was more discreet and secret than ordinarily other women are. Above all, she was exceedingly religious and devout: and therefore seeing herself without hope of children, and now well stricken in years, she made it her business, as I did, to think of God, and to give ourselves to the works of charity and mercy.

"Before the time wherein I wrote this discourse, which

was at the latter end of the year of our Lord 1413, after
the death of my faithful companion, whose loss I cannot
but lament all the days of my life, she and I had already
founded, and endowed with revenues, fourteen hospitals,
three chapels, and seven churches, in the city of Paris, all
which we had new built from the ground, and enriched
with great gifts and revenues, with many reparations in
their churchyards. We also have done at Boulogne about
as much as we have done at Paris, not to speak of the
charitable acts which we both did to particular poor
people, principally to widows and orphans, whose names
should I divulge, with the largeness of the charity, and
the way and manner of doing it, as my reward would then
be only in this world, so neither could it be pleasing to the
persons to whom we did it.

" Building, therefore, these hospitals, chapels, churches,
and churchyards in the city, I caused to be depicted under
the said fourth arch the most true and essential marks or
signs of this art, yet under veils, types, and hieroglyphic
covertures, in imitation of those things which are contained
in the gilded book of Abraham the Jew; demonstrating to
the wise, and men of understanding, the direct and perfect
way of operation, and lineary work of the philosophers'
stone. Which being perfected by any one, takes away
from him the root of all sin and evil, which is covetousness,
changing his evil into good, and making him liberal,
courteous, religious, devout, and fearing God, however
wicked he was before. For from thenceforward he is
continually ravished with the goodness of God, and with
His grace and mercy, which he has obtained from the
fountain of Eternal Goodness, with the profoundness of
His divine and adorable power, and with the consideration
of His admirable works."

According to Langlet du Fresnoy, the evidence of these

things remained in the year 1742. In the cemetery of the
Holy Innocents stood the arch built by Flamel with the
hieroglpyhic figures upon it. In two niches, without the
arch and on the cemetery side, were statues of St James
and St John. Below that of St John was the figure of
Flamel himself, reading in a book, with a Gothic N. F. to
mark his name. The progression of the colours in the
order of the process, originally represented on the wall,
was, however, effaced.

In the same cemetery was a charnel house, or receptacle
for the skulls and bones disinterred in the digging of new
graves. Upon one of the pillars of this charnel there was
a Gothic N. F., with this inscription :—

> *Ce charnier fut fait & donné à l'Eglise,*
> *Pour l'amour de Dieu, l'an* 1399.

The second of these evidences was upon the Marivaux
door of the Church of Saint Jacques-la-Boucherie, where
on the left side at entering was the figure of Flamel, kneeling at the feet of St James, with a Gothic N. upon the
pedestal. The figure of Perrenelle was represented on the
opposite side, kneeling at the feet of St John, the pedestal
bearing a Gothic P.

The third evidence was in the street of Notre Dame,
at the portal of Genevieve of Arden. There Flamel's statue
was to be seen in a niche, kneeling with a desk at his
side, looking towards St James. There was a Gothic
N. F. below and the inscription, " This portal was built in
1402, by the alms of many." Flamel is supposed to have
concealed in this manner that he was the principal donor,
but the figure may have been erected to his memory.

The fourth and final evidence was in the street of the
cemetery of St Nicholas of the Fields, where there was the
wall of an unfinished hospital with figures engraven on the
stone and the initials of Flamel.

After the death of Perrenelle the bereaved adept is supposed to have prepared for posterity several works on the supreme science which had enriched him:—*Le Livre des Figures Hieroglyphiques; Le Sommaire Philosophique*, written in verse after the manner of the *Roman de la Rose; Trois Traités de la Transformation Metallique*, also in rhymed· verse·; *Le Desir Désiré, ou Trésor de Philosophie; Le Grand Eclaircissement de la Pierre Philosophale pour la Transmutation de tous Métaux; La Musique Chimique; Annotationes in D. Zacharmin*, &c.

Approaching near the end of his life, and having no children, he chose his burial place in the parish church of St Jacques-la-Boucherie, before the crucifix. To this end he made a contract with the wardens of the church, which is mentioned in his testament. He then disposed of his property and goods to the church and to the poor, as may be seen in his will, which is lodged in the archives of St Jacques. It is dated the 22nd November 1416, and begins thus:—" To all those to whom these present letters shall come, I, Annegny du Castel, chevalier, counsellor chambellan of the King, our Sire, Keeper of the Prevot of Paris, greeting : Know ye, that before Hugues de la Barre and Jean de la Noe, notary clerks of the King, at the Chatelet, was established personally, Nicholas Flamel, scrivener, sound in body and mind, speaking clearly, with good and true understanding," &c. It fills four sheets of parchment, which are sewed one to the end of the other, like the rolls of ancient writing. It contains thirty-four articles; in the twentieth he bequeaths to his relations the sum of forty livres. He lived three years after making this will, dying about 1419.

Hostile criticism has endeavoured to destroy the testimony which the history of Flamel affords to the reality of transmutation, and has adopted various means. It has attempted to disprove his wealth by reducing his munificence, representing him simply as an honest bourgeois, who, thanks to his economy and his assiduity, acquired a comfortable competence, which a childless condition enabled him to devote to works of benevolence, and to the erection of public buildings on a moderate scale. The alchemical testaments and treatises attributed to him are condemned one and all as absolutely spurious. The chief expositor of this view is the Abbé L. Vilain in his *Essai sur une Histoire de Saint-Jacques-la-Boucherie*, published in duodecimo at Paris, in 1758, and again in a *Histoire Critique de Nicolas Flamel et de Pernel sa Femme*, Paris, 1782, &c.

It must be granted out of hand that all the alchemical compositions which have passed under the name of Flamel are open to more or less suspicion, and some are undoubtedly forgeries. The work on metallic transmutation, which is the earliest traceable treatise, was unheard of till a hundred and forty-three years after the death of its accredited author. It was published in the year 1561 by Jacques Goharry. *Le Grand Eclaircissement* first saw the light in 1628, when the editor, who apparently abounded in Flamel manuscripts, promised the publication in addition of *La Joie Parfaite de Moi, Nicolas Flamel, et de Pernelle, ma Femme*, which has not, however, appeared.

On the other hand, there are strong arguments for the genuineness of the *Trésor de Philosophie*. "There exists in the *Bibliothèque du Roi*," says M. Auguste Vallet, "a small manuscript book, *grossement relié*, according to all appearance belonging to the end of the fourteenth century, and which treats of alchemical operations. It commences with these words :—

" 'Excipit the True Practice of the Noble Science of Alchemy, the desired desire, and the prize unappraisable, compiled from all the philosophers, and drawn out of ancient works.'

"It teaches the manner of accomplishing the *Magnum Opus* by the aid of successive operations, which are termed *Lavures* in this treatise. On the last leaf of the manuscript is the following inscription written by the same hand as the rest of the text :—' The present book is of and belonging to Nicolas Flamel, of the Parish Saint-Jacques-de-la-Boucherie, who has written and illuminated it with his own hand.' "

With regard to the extent of the ,scrivener's resources, the genuine testament of Pernelle, dated 1399, and the endowments of hospitals and churches which undoubtedly took place on a scale of great munificence, are a sufficient evidence that he was an exceedingly wealthy man.

Other critics, including Louis Figuier, admit the fact of his riches, but enlarge upon the remunerative nature of a scrivener's occupation previous to the invention of printing, and upon the careful frugality of the supposed alchemist ; but in the teeth of their own theory they are obliged to admit that Flamel did become a student of alchemy, that the hieroglyphics, figures, and emblems in the Cemetery of the Holy Innocents are evidence of this fact ; that, unlike most followers of Hermes, he was not impoverished by his experiments ; and that he fostered the report that his wealth was in the main a result of his possession of the mysterious book of Abraham, by which he had been able to compose the philosophical stone.

Gabriel Naudé, who detested magic, and seems to have despised alchemy, vilifying the possessors of both of these sciences alike, accounts for the riches of Flamel 'by asserting that he managed affairs for the Jews, and upon their banishment from the kingdom of France, and the confiscation of their property for the king, " he, knowing the sums due by several individuals, compromised, by receiving a part, which they paid him to prevent his giving information which would oblige them to surrender it entirely."

This explanation of the source of Flamel's riches is a purely unfounded assertion. If we carefully examine history, there were three expulsions of the Jews from France between 1300 and 1420. They were banished in 1308, were soon after allowed to return, and were again banished in 1320. These persecutions occurred before the birth of Flamel. The Jews were re-established by Charles V. in 1364, and they remained in quiet until the riots which occurred in Paris in 1380, at the beginning of the reign of Charles VI., when the people rose up against the Jews, committing great outrages and demanding their expulsion. The sedition, however, was quelled, and the Jews protected until 1393, when, upon several charges preferred against them, they were enjoined to quit France, or else become Christians. The historian Mezeray says that some of them chose rather to quit their religion than the kingdom, but others sold their goods and retired. Thus it appears that the only expulsion of the Jews which could agree with Naudé's surmise was without the confiscation of their property, and, therefore, could not give Flamel the opportunity alleged, if, indeed, it were reasonable to suppose that all the Parisian Israelites entrusted their affairs to a single person, when it does not appear that necessity required such an agency. There is, therefore, no reason to suppose that Flamel was enriched by the property of the Jews, or that those who owed them money compounded with Flamel, lest he should denounce them to the king.*

.* According to Louis Figuier, there were two minor persecutions of the Jews, one in 1346, when Flamel was merely a boy, and the other in 1354, when he was scarcely established in business.

Thus the theories of hostile criticism break down before impartial examination, and to whatever source we may choose to ascribe the wealth of Nicholas Flamel, we have no reason to question his integrity, nor to deny the explanation of the alchemists, except upon the *à priori* ground of the impossibility of transmutation.

The divine gift which was so fortunate a possession to Flamel is supposed to have been a curse to his descendants. He is reported to have given some of the transmuting powder to M. Perrier, a nephew of Perrenelle. From him it descended to Dr Perrier, and was found among his effects at his death by his grandson, Dubois. The prudence and moderation that accompanied the gift to the Perriers was not found in Dubois. He exhibited the sacred miracle to improper persons, says an anonymous writer on alchemy, and was brought before Louis XIII., in whose presence he made gold of base metal, and this gold augmented its weight in the cupel. The consequence of this generosity was an infamous death. The vanity of Dubois was in proportion to his imprudence. He fancied that he could make or augment the powder, and promised to do so, but without success. It seems that he was, consequently, suspected of withholding the art from the king, a circumstance sufficient in politics to justify strong measures, lest the possessor of the sinews of war should go over to the enemy.

Whatever were the charges against Dubois, he was hanged, and his fate should be a proof, says the writer already quoted, that a science producing unbounded riches is the greatest misfortune to those who are unfitted and unprepared to manage the dangerous trust with discretion.

After the death of Flamel, many persons supposed that there must be doubtless some buried treasures in the house which he had inhabited during so many years, and in which all his Hermetical triumphs had been performed. This opinion existed in all its strength, at least in the mind of one individual, so late as the year 1576, when a stranger applied to the Prévôt of Paris, and stated that he had been entrusted by a deceased friend with certain sums for the restoration of Flamel's house. As the building was exceedingly dilapidated, the magistrates availed themselves of the opportunity, and repairs were begun under the direction of delegates of the works of Saint-Jacques-de-la-Boucherie. The true object of the stranger soon became evident by the determination with which he sought to lay bare the whole foundations of the house, which was ransacked from top to bottom in search of the treasures it was supposed to conceal. No discoveries rewarded the zeal of the investigation, which ended in the sudden disappearance of the stranger, without paying for the operations which he had caused to be set on foot.

As a completion to the history of Flamel, it may be entertaining to quote an extraordinary account which is seriously narrated by Paul Lucas in his " Journey through Asia Minor."

" I was at Bronosa, in Natolia, and going to take the air with a person of distinction, came to a little mosque, which was adorned with gardens and fountains for a public walk ; we were quickly introduced into a cloister, where we found four dervishes, who received us with all imaginable civility, and desired us to partake of what they were eating. We were told, what we soon found to be true, that they were all persons of the greatest worth and learning ; one of them, who said he was of Usbec Tartary, appeared to be more accomplished than the rest, and I believe verily he spoke all the principal languages of the world. After we had conversed in Turkish, he asked me if I could speak Latin, Spanish, or Italian. I told him, if he pleased, to speak to me in Italian; but he soon discovered by my accent that it was not my mother-tongue, and asked me frankly what country I came from? As soon as he knew that I was a native of France, he spoke to me in as good French as if he had been brought up at Paris. 'How long, sir,' said I, 'did you stay in France?' He replied he had never been there, but that he had a great inclination to undertake the journey.

"I did all in my power to strengthen that resolution, and to convince him that France was the nursery of the learned, and its king a patron of the sciences, who defrayed the expense of my travels for collecting notices of antiquities, drawings of monuments, correcting maps, and making a collection of ancient coins, manuscripts, &c., all of which he seemed to approve civilly. Our conversation being ended, the dervishes brought us to their house, at the foot of the mountain, where, having drank coffee, I took my leave, but with a promise, however, that I would shortly come and see them again.

"On the 10th, the dervish whom I took for an Usbec came to pay me a visit. I shewed him all the manuscripts I had bought, and he assured me they were very valuable, and written by great authors. He was a man every way extraordinary in learning; and in external appearance he seemed to be about thirty years old, but from his discourse I was persuaded he had lived a century.

"He told me he was one of seven friends, who travelled to perfect their studies, and, every twenty years, met in a place previously appointed. I perceived that Bronosa was the place of their present meeting, and that four of them had arrived. Religion and natural philosophy took up our thoughts by turns; and at last we fell upon chemistry, alchemy, and the Cabala. I told him all these, and especially the philosophers' stone, were regarded by most men of sense as mere fictions.

" 'That,' replied he, 'should not surprise you; the sage hears the ignorant without being shocked, but does not for that reason sink his understanding to the same level. When I speak of a sage, I mean one who sees all things die and revive without concern : he has more riches in his power than the greatest king, but lives temperately, above the power of events.'

" Here I stopped him :—' With all these fine maxims, the sage dies as well as other people.' ' Alas ! ' said he, ' I perceive you are unacquainted with sublime science. Such a one as I describe dies indeed, for death is inevitable, but he ·does not die before the utmost limits of. his mortal existence. Hereditary disease and weakness reduce the life of man, but the sage, by the use of the true medicine, can ward off whatever may hinder or impair the animal functions for a thousand years.'

" Surprised at all I heard, ' And would you persuade me,' said I, ' that all who possessed the philosophers' stone have lived a thousand years ? ' He replied gravely :— ' Without doubt every one might ; it depends entirely on themselves.' At last I took the liberty of naming the celebrated Flamel, who, it was said, possessed the philosophers' stone, yet was certainly dead. He smiled at my simplicity, and asked with an air of mirth :—' Do you really believe this ? No, no, my friend, Flamel is still living ; neither he nor his wife are dead. It is not above three years since I left both the one and the other in the Indies ; he is one of my best friends.' Whereupon he told me the history of Flamel, as he heard it from himself, the same as I had read in his book, until at last when Charles VI., who was then upon the throne, sent M. Cramoisi, a magistrate, and his master of requests, to enquire from Flamel the origin of his riches, when the latter at once saw the danger he was in. Having sent her into Switzerland to await his coming, he spread a report of his wife's death, had her funeral celebrated, and in a few years ordered his own coffin to be interred. Since that time they have both lived a philosophic life, sometimes in one country, sometimes in another. This is the true history, and not that which is believed at Paris, where there are very few who ever had the least glimpse of true wisdom.' "

According to the " Treasure of Philosophy," alchemy as a science consists in the knowledge of the four elements of philosophers, which are not to be identified with the vulgar so-called elements, and which are convertible one into another. The true *prima materia* is mercury, prepared and congealed in the bowels of the earth by the mediation of the heat of sulphur. This is the sperm and semen of all metals, which, like other created things, are capable of a growth and multiplication that may be continued even to infinity. The first step in transmutation is the reduction of the metals worked upon into their first mercurial matter, and this reduction is the subject of the whole treatise.

It does not appear that the alchemical works attributed to Nicholas Flamel have added anything to our knowledge of chemistry. On the other hand, it is perfectly clear from his history that the physical object of Alchemy was the end which he kept in view, and that also which he is supposed to have attained.

WISDOM has various means for making its way into the heart of man. Sometimes a prophet comes forward and speaks. Or a sect of mystics receives the teaching of a philosophy, like rain on a summer evening, gathers it in and spreads it abroad with love. Or it may happen that a charlatan, performing tricks to astonish men, may produce, perhaps without knowing it himself, a ray of real light with his dice and magic mirrors. In the fourteenth century the pure truth of the masters was transmitted by a book. This book fell into the hands of precisely the man who was destined to receive it; and he, with the help of the text and the hieroglyphic diagrams which taught the transmutation of metals into gold, accomplished the transmutation of his soul, which is a far rarer and more wonderful operation.

Thanks to the amazing book of Abraham the Jew all the hermetists of the following centuries had the opportunity of admiring an example of a perfect life, that of Nicolas Flamel, the man who received the book. After his death or disappearance many students and alchemists who had devoted their lives to the search for the philosopher's stone despaired because they had not in their possession the wonderful book in which was contained the secret of gold and of eternal life. But their despair was unnecessary. The secret had become alive. The magic formulæ had become incarnate in the actions of a man. No ingot of virgin gold melted in the crucibles could, in colour or purity, attain the beauty of the wise bookseller's pious life.

There is nothing legendary about the life of Nicolas Flamel. The Bibliothèque Nationale contains works copied in his hand and original works written by him. All the official documents relating to his life have been found, his marriage contract, his deeds of gift, his will. His history rests solidly on those substantial material proofs for which men clamour if they are to believe in the most obvious things (whenever those obvious things are also beautiful). To this indisputably authentic history legend has added a few flowers. But in every spot where the flowers of legend grow, underneath there is the solid earth of truth.

Whether Nicolas Flamel was born at Pontoise or somewhere else, a question which historians have investigated with extreme attention, seems to me to be entirely without importance. It is enough to know that towards the middle of the fourteenth century he was carrying on the trade of a bookseller and had a stall backing on to the columns of Saint-Jacques la Boucherie.

It was not a big stall, for it measured only two feet by two and a half. However, it grew. He bought a house in the old rue de Marivaux and used the ground-floor for his business. Copyists and illuminators did their work there. He himself gave a few writing lessons and taught nobles who could only sign their names with a cross. One of the copyists or illuminators acted also as a servant to him.

Nicolas Flamel married Pernelle, a good-looking,

intelligent widow, slightly older than himself and the possessor of a little property.

Every man meets once in his life the woman with whom he could live in peace and harmony. For Nicolas Flamel, Pernelle was that woman. Over and above her natural qualities she had another which is still rarer. She was the only woman in the history of humanity who was capable of keeping a secret all her life without revealing it to everybody in confidence.

The story of Nicolas Flamel is the story of a book. The secret made its appearance with the book. Neither the death of its possessors nor the lapse of centuries led to the complete discovery of the secret.

Nicolas Flamel had acquired some knowledge of the hermetic art. The ancient alchemy of the Egyptians and the Greeks which flourished among the Arabs had, thanks to them, penetrated to Christian countries. Nicolas Flamel did not, of course, regard alchemy as a mere vulgar search for the means of making gold. For every exalted mind the finding of the philosopher's stone was the finding of the essential secret of Nature, the secret of her unity and her laws, the possession of perfect wisdom. Flamel dreamed of sharing in this wisdom. His ideal was the highest that man can attain. And he knew that it could be realised through a book. For the secret of the philosopher's stone had already been found and transcribed in symbolic form. Somewhere it existed. It was in the hands of unknown sages who lived somewhere unknown. But how difficult it was for a small Paris bookseller to get into touch with those sages.

Nothing, then, has changed since the fourteenth

century. In our day also many men strive desperately towards an ideal, the path which they know but cannot climb ; and they hope to win the magic formula (which will make them new beings) from some miraculous visit or from a book written expressly for them. But the visitor does not come and the book is not written.

But for Nicolas Flamel the book *was* written. Perhaps because a bookseller is better situated than other people to receive a unique book ; perhaps because the strength of his desire organised events without his knowledge, so that the book came when it was time.

So strong was his desire, that the coming of the book was preceded by a dream, which shows that this wise and well-balanced bookseller had a tendency to mysticism.

Nicolas Flamel dreamed one night that an angel stood before him. The angel, who was radiant and winged like all angels, held a book in his hands and uttered these words, which were to remain in the memory of the hearer :

" Look well at this book. At first you will understand nothing in it, neither you nor any other man. But one day you will see in it that which no other man will be able to see."

Flamel stretched out his hand to receive the present from the angel, and the whole scene disappeared in the golden light of dreams.

Some time after that the dream was partly realised.

One day, when Nicolas Flamel was alone in his shop, an unknown man in need of money appeared with a manuscript to sell. Flamel was no doubt tempted to

receive him with disdainful arrogance, as do the book-
sellers of our day when some poor student offers to sell
them part of his library.   But the moment he saw the
book he recognised it as the book which the angel
had held out to him, and he paid two florins for it without
bargaining.

The book appeared to him indeed resplendent and
instinct with divine virtue.   It had a very old binding
of worked copper, on which were engraved curious
diagrams and certain characters, some of which were
Greek and others in a language he could not decipher.
The leaves of the book were not made of parchment,
like those he was accustomed to copy and bind.   They
were made of the bark of young trees and were covered
with very clear writing done with an iron point.   These
leaves were divided into groups of seven and consisted
of three parts separated by a page without writing, but
containing a diagram which was quite unintelligible to
Flamel.   On the first page were written words to the
effect that the author of the manuscript was Abraham
the Jew, prince, priest, Levite, astrologer and philosopher.
Then followed great curses and threats against anyone
who set eyes on it unless he was either a priest or a scribe.
The word *maranatha*, which was many times repeated
on every page, intensified the awe-inspiring character of
the text and diagrams.   But most impressive of all was
the patined gold of the edges of the book, and the atmos-
phere of hallowed antiquity that there was about it.

Maranatha ! Yet Nicolas Flamel considered that
being a scribe he might read the book without fear.   He
felt that the secret of life and of death, the secret of the
unity of Nature, the secret of the duty of the wise man,

had been concealed behind the symbol of the diagrams and formulæ in the text by an initiate long since dead. He was aware that it is a rigid law for initiates that they must not reveal their knowledge, because if it is good and fruitful for the intelligent, it is bad for ordinary men. As Jesus has clearly expressed it, pearls must not be given as food to swine.

He had the pearl in his hands. It was for him to rise in the scale of man in order to be worthy to understand its purity. He must have had in his heart a hymn of thanksgiving to Abraham the Jew, whose name was unknown to him, but who had thought and laboured in past centuries and whose wisdom he was now inheriting. He must have pictured him a bald old man with a hooked nose, wearing the wretched robe of his race and writing in some dark ghetto, in order that the light of his thought might not be lost. And he must have vowed to solve the riddle, to re-kindle the light, to be patient and faithful, like the Jew who had died in the flesh but lived eternally in his manuscript.

Nicolas Flamel had studied the art of transmutation. He was in touch with all the learned men of his day. Manuscripts dealing with chemistry have been found, notably that of Almasatus, which were part of his personal library. He had knowledge of the symbols of which the alchemists made habitual use. But those which he saw in the book of Abraham the Jew remained dumb for him. In vain he copied some of the mysterious pages and set them out in his shop, in the hope that some visitor conversant with the Cabala would help him to solve the problem. He met with nothing but the laughter of sceptics and the ignorance of pseudo-scholars

—just as he would to-day if he showed the book of Abraham the Jew either to pretentious occultists or to the Académie des Inscriptions et Belles Lettres.

For twenty-one years he pondered the hidden meaning of the book. That is not long. He is favoured among men for whom twenty-one years are enough to enable him to find the key of life.

A T the end of twenty-one years Nicolas Flamel had developed in himself sufficient wisdom and strength to hold out against the storm of light involved by the coming of truth to the heart of man. Only then did events group themselves harmoniously according to his will and allow him to realise his desire. For everything good and great that happens to a man is the result of the co-ordination of his own voluntary effort and a malleable fate.

No one in Paris could help Nicolas Flamel to understand the book. Now this book had been written by a Jew, and part of its text was in ancient Hebrew. The Jews had recently been driven out of France by persecution. Nicolas Flamel knew that many of these Jews had migrated to Spain. In towns such as Malaga and Granada, which were still under the enlightened dominion of the Arabs, there lived prosperous communities of Jews and flourishing synagogues, in which scholars and doctors were bred. Many Jews from the Christian towns of Spain took advantage of the tolerance extended by the Moorish kings and went to Granada to learn. There they copied Plato and Aristotle and returned home to spread abroad the knowledge of the ancients and of the Arab masters.

Nicolas Flamel thought that in Spain he might meet some erudite Cabalist who would translate the book of

Abraham for him. Travelling was difficult, and without a strong armed escort it was possible only for a pilgrim. Flamel alleged therefore a vow to St James of Compostela, the patron saint of his parish. This was also a means of concealing from his neighbours and friends the real purpose of his journey. The wise and faithful Pernelle was the only person who was aware of his real plans. He put on the pilgrim's attire and shell-adorned hat, took the staff, which ensured a certain measure of safety to a traveller in Christian countries, and started off for Galicia.

Since he was a prudent man and did not wish to expose the precious manuscript to the risks of travel, he contented himself with taking with him a few carefully copied pages, which he hid in his modest baggage.

Nicolas Flamel has not recounted the adventures that befell him on his journey. Possibly he had none—it may be that adventures happen only to those who want to have them. He has told us merely that he went first to fulfil his vow to St James. Then he wandered about Spain, trying to get into relations with learned Jews. But they were suspicious of Christians, particularly of the French, who had expelled them from their country. Besides, he had not much time. He had to remember Pernelle waiting for him, and his shop, which was being managed only by his servants. To a man of over fifty on his first distant journey the silent voice of his home makes a powerful appeal every evening.

In discouragement he started his homeward journey. His way lay through León, where he stopped for the night at an inn and happened to sup at the same table as a French merchant from Boulogne who was travelling on business. This merchant inspired him with confidence and he whispered a few words to him of his wish to find a learned Jew. By a lucky chance the French merchant was in relations with a certain Maestro Canches, an old man who lived at León, immersed in his books. Nothing was easier than to introduce this Maestro Canches to Nicolas Flamel, who decided to make one more attempt before leaving Spain.

I can picture the beauty of the scene when the profane merchant of Boulogne has left them, and the two men are face to face. The gates of the ghetto close. Maestro Canches' only thought is by a few polite words to rid himself as quickly as he can of this French bookseller, who has deliberately dulled the light in his eye and clothed himself in mediocrity; for the prudent traveller passes unnoticed. Flamel speaks, reticently at first. He admires the knowledge of the Jews. Thanks to his trade he has read a great many books. At last he timidly lets fall a name, which hitherto has aroused not a spark of interest in anyone to whom he has spoken—the name of Abraham the Jew, prince, priest, Levite, astrologer and philosopher. Suddenly Flamel sees the eyes of the feeble old man before him light up. Maestro Canches has heard of Abraham the Jew. He was a great master of the wandering race, perhaps the most venerable of all the sages who studied the mysteries of the Cabala, a higher initiate, one of those who rise the higher the better they succeed in remaining unknown. His book existed and disappeared centuries ago, but tradition says it has never been destroyed, that it is passed from hand to hand and that it always reaches the man whose destiny it is to receive it. Maestro Canches has dreamed all his life long of finding it. He is very old, close to death, and now the hope which he has almost given up is near realisation. The night goes by, and there is a light round the two heads bent over their work. Maestro Canches is translating Hebrew of the time of Moses. He is explaining symbols which originated in Chaldæa. How the years fall from these two men, inspired by their belief in truth !

But the few pages that Flamel had brought were not enough to allow the secret to be revealed. Maestro Canches made up his mind at once to accompany Flamel to Paris. His extreme old age was an obstacle. That he would defy. Jews were not allowed in France. F would be converted. For many years he had been above all religions. The two men, united by an indissoluble bond, started off along the Spanish roads.

The ways of nature are mysterious. The nearer Maestro Canches came to the realisation of his dream, the more precarious became his health ; and the breath of life weakened in him. O God ! he prayed, grant me the days I need, and that I may cross the threshold of death only when I possess the liberating secret by which darkness becomes light and flesh spirit !

But the prayer was not heard. The inflexible law had appointed the hour of the old man's death. He fell ill at Orleans and in spite of all Flamel's care died seven days later. As he had been converted and Flamel did not wish to be suspected of having brought a Jew into France, he had him piously buried in the church of Sainte-Croix and had masses said for him ; for he rightly thought that a soul which had striven for so pure an aim and had passed at the moment of fruition could not rest in the realm of disembodied spirits.

Flamel continued his journey and reached Paris, where he found Pernelle, his shop, his copyists, his manuscripts. He laid aside his pilgrim's staff. But now everything was changed. It was with a joyous heart that he went his daily journey from house to shop, that he gave writing lessons to illiterates and discussed hermetic science with the educated. From natural prudence he continued to feign ignorance, in which he succeeded all the more easily because knowledge was within him. What Maestro Canches had already taught him in deciphering a few pages of the book of Abraham the Jew was sufficient to allow of his understanding the whole book. He spent three years more in searching and in completing his knowledge, but at the end of this period the transmutation was accomplished. Having learned what materials it was necessary to put together beforehand, he followed strictly the method of Abraham the Jew and changed a half-pound of mercury first into silver, and then into virgin gold. And he accomplished the same transmutation in his soul. From his passions, mixed in an invisible crucible, the substance of the eternal spirit emerged.

FROM this point the little bookseller became rich. He bought houses, endowed churches. But he did not use his riches to increase his personal comfort or to satisfy his vanity. He altered nothing in his modest life. With Pernelle, who had helped him in his search for the philosopher's stone, he devoted his life to helping his fellow-men. " Husband and wife lavished succour on the poor, founded hospitals, built or repaired cemeteries, restored the front of Sainte-Geneviève des Ardents and endowed the institution of the Quinze-Vingts, the blind inmates of which, in memory of this fact, came every year to the church of Saint-Jacques la Boucherie to pray for their benefactor, a practice which continued until 1789."*

At the same time that he was learning how to make gold out of any material, he acquired the wisdom of despising it in his heart. Thanks to the book of Abraham the Jew he had risen above the satisfaction of his senses and the turmoil of his passions. He knew that man attains immortality only by the victory of spirit over matter, by essential purification, by the transmutation of the human into the divine. He devoted the last part of his life to what Christians call the working out of their salvation.

He attained his object without fasting or asceticism,

* Louis Figuier.

keeping the unimportant place that destiny had assigned him, continuing to copy manuscripts, buying and selling, in his little shop in the rue Saint-Jacques la Boucherie. For him there was no more mystery about the cemetery of the Innocents, which was near his house and under the arcades of which he liked to walk in the evenings. If he had the vaults and monuments restored at his own expense, it was nothing more than compliance with the custom of his time. He knew that the dead who had been laid to rest there were not concerned with stones and inscriptions and that they would return, when their hour came, in different forms, to perfect themselves and die anew. He knew the trifling extent to which he could help them. He had no temptation to divulge the secret which had been entrusted to him through the book, for he was able to measure the lowest degree of virtue necessary for the possession of it, and he knew that the revelation of the secret to an undeveloped soul only increased the imperfection of that soul.

And when he was illuminating a manuscript and putting in with a fine brush a touch of sky-blue into the eye of an angel, or of white into a wing, no smile played on his grave face, for he knew that pictures are useful to children; moreover, it is possible that beautiful fantasies which are pictured with love and sincerity may become realities in the dream of death.

Though he knew how to make gold, Nicolas Flamel made it only three times in the whole of his life; and then not for himself, for he never changed his way of life; he did it only to mitigate the evils which he saw around him. And this is the touchstone which allows us to recognise that he really attained the state of adept.

This touchstone can be used by everyone and at all times. To distinguish a man's superiority, there is but a single sign, a practical—and not an alleged—contempt for riches. However great may be a man's active virtues or the radiant power of his intelligence, if they are accompanied by the love of money which most eminent men possess, it is certain that they are tainted with baseness. What they create under the hypocritical pretext of good, will bear within it the seeds of decay. Unselfishness alone is creative, and it alone can help to raise man.

Flamel's generous gifts aroused curiosity and even jealousy. It seemed amazing that a poor bookseller should found almshouses and hospitals, should build houses with low rents, churches and convents. Rumours reached the ears of the king, Charles VI, who ordered Cramoisi, a member of the Council of State, to investigate the matter. But thanks to Flamel's prudence and reticence the result of the inquiries was favourable to him.

The rest of Flamel's life passed without special event. It was the life of a scholar. He went from his house in the rue de Marivaux to his shop. He walked in the cemetery of the Innocents, for the imagination of death was pleasant to him. He handled beautiful parchments. He illuminated missals. He smiled on Pernelle as she grew old, and he knew that life holds few better things than the peace of daily work and a calm affection.

Pernelle died first. Nicolas Flamel reached the age of eighty. He spent the last years of his life writing books on alchemy. He carefully settled his affairs and how he was to be buried, at the end of the nave of Saint-Jacques la Boucherie. The tomb-stone to be laid over his body had already been made. On this stone, in the middle of various figures, there was carved a sun above a key and a closed book. It was the symbol of his life.* His death, to which he joyfully looked forward, was as circumspect and as perfect as his life.

As it is equally useful to study men's weaknesses as their finest qualities, we may mark Flamel's weakness. This sage, who attached importance only to the immortality of his soul and despised the ephemeral form of the body, was inspired as he grew old with a strange taste for the sculptural representation of his body and face. Whenever he had a church built, or even restored, he requested the sculptor to represent him, piously kneeling, in a corner of the pediment of the façade. He had himself twice sculptured on an arch in the cemetery of the Innocents, once as he was in his youth, and once old and infirm. When he had a new house built (called " the house with the big gable ") in the rue de Montmorency, on the outskirts of Paris, eleven saints were carved on the front, but a side door was surmounted with a bust of Flamel.

It seems, then, that however great a man's wisdom, however far he carries his desire to break away from his physical form, he cannot prevent himself cherishing a secret affection for that unbeautiful form, and insists that the memory of what he proclaimed contemptible should nevertheless be perpetuated in stone.

* Flamel's tomb-stone is in the Musée de Cluny, in Paris.

THE bones of sages seldom rest in peace in their grave. Perhaps Nicolas Flamel knew this and tried to protect his remains by ordering a tomb-stone of great weight and by having a religious service held for him twelve times a year. But these precautions were useless.

Hardly was Flamel dead when the report of his alchemical powers and of his concealment somewhere of an enormous quantity of gold spread through Paris and the world. Everyone who was seeking the famous projection powder, which turns all substances into gold, came prowling round all the places where he had lived in the hope of finding a minute portion of the precious powder. It was said also that the symbolical figures which he had had sculptured on various monuments gave, for those who could decipher it, the formula of the philosopher's stone. There was not a single alchemist but came in pilgrimage to study the sacred science on the stones of Saint-Jacques la Boucherie or the cemetery of the Innocents. The sculptures and inscriptions were broken off at night and removed. The cellars of his house were searched and the walls examined. " Towards the middle of the sixteenth century a man who had a well-known name and good credentials, which were no doubt fictitious, presented himself before the parish

board of Saint-Jacques la Boucherie. He said he wished
to carry out the vow of a dead friend, a pious alchemist,
who, on his death-bed, had given him a sum of money
with which to repair Flamel's house. The board accepted
the offer. The unknown man had the cellars ransacked
under the pretext of strengthening the foundations;
wherever he saw a hieroglyph he found some reason for
knocking down the wall at that point. Undeceived at
last, he disappeared, forgetting to pay the work-
men."*

A Capuchin friar and a German baron are said to have
discovered in the house some stone phials full of a reddish
powder, no doubt the projection powder. By the
seventeenth century the various houses which had
belonged to Flamel were despoiled of their ornaments
and decorations, and there was nothing of them left but
the four bare walls.

But what had happened to the book of Abraham the
Jew ? Nicolas Flamel had bequeathed his papers and
library to a nephew named Perrier, who was interested
in alchemy and of whom he was very fond. Absolutely
nothing is known of Perrier. He no doubt benefited by
his uncle's teachings and spent a sage's life in the
munificent obscurity which Flamel prized so dearly, but
had not been able altogether to maintain during the
last years of his life. For two centuries the precious
heritage was handed down from father to son, without
anything being heard of it. Traces of it are found again
in the reign of Louis XIII. A descendant of Flamel,
named Dubois, who must still have possessed a supply
of the projection powder, threw off the wise reserve of

* Albert Poisson, *Nicolas Flamel*.

his ancestors and used the powder to dazzle his contemporaries. In the presence of the king he changed leaden balls with it into gold. As a result of this experiment he had many interviews with Cardinal de Richelieu, who wished to extract his secret. Dubois, who possessed the powder but was unable to understand either Flamel's manuscripts or the book of Abraham the Jew, could tell him nothing and was imprisoned at Vincennes. It was found that he had committed certain offences in the past, and this enabled Richelieu to get him condemned to death and confiscate his property for his own benefit. At the same time the proctor of the Châtelet, no doubt by order of Richelieu, seized the houses that Flamel had owned and had them searched from top to bottom.

It was impossible to hide altogether, though the attempt was made, the profanation of the church of Saint-Jacques la Boucherie. Robbers made their way in during the night, lifted Flamel's tombstone and broke his coffin. It was after this that the rumour was first spread that the coffin had been found empty, and that it had never contained the body of Flamel, who was supposed to be still alive.

Richelieu took possession of the book of Abraham the Jew. He built a laboratory in the château of Rueil, which he often visited to read through the master's manuscripts and to try to interpret the sacred hieroglyphs. But that which a sage like Flamel had been able to understand only after twenty-one years of meditation was not likely to be at once accessible to a statesman like Richelieu. Knowledge of the mutations of matter, of life and death, is more complex than the art of writing tragedies or administering a kingdom. Richelieu's search gave no result.

On the death of the cardinal all traces of the book* were lost, or rather, all traces of the text, for the diagrams have often been reproduced. It must have been copied, for in the seventeenth century the author of the *Trésor des recherches et antiquités gauloises* made a journey to Milan to see a copy which belonged to the Seigneur of Cabrières.

It has now disappeared. Perhaps a copy or the original itself rests under the dust of some provincial library ; and it may be that a wise fate will send it at the proper time to a man who has the patience to ponder it, the knowledge to interpret it, the wisdom not to divulge it.

But the mystery of the story of Flamel, which seemed to have come to an end, was revived in the seventeenth century.

Louis XIV sent an archæologist, named Paul Lucas, on a mission to the East. He was to study antiquities and bring back any inscriptions or documents which might help forward the modest scientific efforts then being made in France. A scholar had in those days to be at the same time both a soldier and an adventurer. Paul Lucas united in himself the qualities of a Salomon Reinach and a Casanova. He was captured by Barbary corsairs, who robbed him, according to his own story, of the treasures he had brought from Greece and Palestine.

* Eliphas Lévi, with the sibylline authoritativeness that is habitual to him, asserts at a venture, without any evidence, that the book of Abraham the Jew is none other than the Ash Mezareph, the commentary on the Cabalistic Sepher Yetzirah.

The most valuable contribution that this official emissary made to science is summarised in the story he tells in his *Voyage dans la Turquie*, which he published in 1719. His account enables men of faith to reconstitute part of the history of the book of Abraham the Jew.

At Broussa Paul Lucas made the acquaintance of a kind of philosopher, who wore Turkish clothes, spoke almost every known language and, in outward appearance, belonged to the type of man of whom it is said that they " have no age." Thanks to his own culture Lucas came to know him fairly well, and this is what he learned. This philosopher was a member of a group of seven philosophers, who belonged to no particular country and travelled all over the world, having no other aim than the search for wisdom and their own development. Every twenty years they met at a pre-determined place, which happened that year to be Broussa. According to him human life ought to have an infinitely longer duration than we admit ; the average length should be a thousand years. A man could live a thousand years if he had knowledge of the philosopher's stone, which, besides being knowledge of the transmutation of metals, was also knowledge of the elixir of life. The sages possessed it and kept it for themselves. In the West there were only a few such sages. Nicolas Flamel had been one of them.

Paul Lucas was astonished that a Turk, whom he had met by chance at Broussa, should be familiar with the story of Flamel. He was still more astonished when the Turk told him how the book of Abraham the Jew had come into Flamel's possession ; for hitherto no one had known this.

" Our sages," he told Lucas, " though there are but few of them in the world, may be met with in any sect. There was a Jew in Flamel's time who had determined not to lose sight of the descendants of his brothers who had taken refuge in France. He had a desire to see them, and in spite of all we could do to dissuade him he went to Paris. He made the acquaintance there of a rabbi who was seeking the philosopher's stone. Our friend became intimate with the rabbi and was able to explain much to him. But before he left the country the rabbi, by an act of black treachery, killed him to get possession of his papers. He was arrested, convicted of this and other crimes and burned alive. The persecution of the Jews began not long afterwards and, as you know, they were expelled from the country."

The book of Abraham, which had been brought by the Eastern sage, was given to Flamel by a Jewish intermediary who did not know its value and was anxious to get rid of it before leaving Paris. But the most amazing thing that Paul Lucas heard was the statement made by the Turk at Broussa that both Flamel and his wife Pernelle were still alive. Having discovered the philosopher's stone he had been able to remain alive in the physical form he possessed at the time of his discovery. Pernelle's and his own funerals and the minute care he bestowed on the arrangements for them had been nothing but clever shams. He had started out for India, the country of the initiates, where he still was.

The publication of Paul Lucas' book created a great sensation. In the seventeenth century, like to-day, there lived discerning men who believed that all truth came out of the East and that there were in India adepts who possessed powers infinitely greater than those which science so parsimoniously metes out to us. For this is a belief that has existed at every period.

Was Nicolas Flamel one of these adepts ? Even if he was, can it reasonably be presumed that he was alive three centuries after his supposed death, by virtue of a deeper study than had yet been made of the life of man and the means of prolonging it ? Is it relevant to compare with Paul Lucas' story another tradition reported by Abbé Vilain, who says that in the seventeenth century Flamel visited M. Desalleurs, the French ambassador to the Sublime Porte ? Every man, according to his feeling for the miraculous, will come to his own conclusion.

I think, myself, that in accordance with the wisdom which he had always shown, Nicolas Flamel, after his discovery of the philosopher's stone, would have had no temptation to evade death ; for he regarded death merely as the transition to a better state. In obeying, without seeking escape, the ancient and simple law which reduces man to dust when the curve of his life is ended, he gave proof of a wisdom which is none the less beautiful for being widespread.

THERE were other adepts after Nicolas Flamel who possessed the secret of the philosopher's stone. We do not know the names of the greatest of them, for the true sign of an adept is his ability to remain unknown. The only trace of them that has come to us is the odour of truth that wisdom leaves behind her. But we know, at any rate partially, the lives of the semi-adepts, who had enough knowledge to practise transmutation, who dimly saw the path to the divine, but remained too human to prevent themselves giving way to their passions. They took part in the work of alchemy with a selfish aim ; and since anything to do with gold unlooses greed and hatred, they were carried away by their own folly and almost all of them perished miserably.

About the middle of the sixteenth century an English lawyer named Talbot who was travelling in Wales, stopped for the night at an inn in a little mountain village. He was wearing a curious cap which encircled his head and face down to the chin. The cap was never removed, and was invariably mentioned when descriptions of him were circulated. This strange head-dress served to hide the place where his ears had been—they had just been cut off in London as a punishment for forgery. The inn-keeper of the little inn where he slept was accustomed to show his customers, as a curiosity, an unintelligible old manuscript. He showed it to Talbot, who was quite well aware of the profit sometimes to be derived from old papers and enquired the origin of the manuscript.

It appeared that a few years before, during the religious wars, some Protestant soldiers had rifled the grave of a Catholic bishop, who, during his lifetime, had been a very rich man. In the grave they found this manuscript and two ivory balls, one red and the other white. They broke the red ball and, finding in it nothing but a dark powder, threw it away. The manuscript and the white ball they had left with the inn-keeper in exchange for a few bottles of wine. While the inn-keeper was showing the manuscript his children were playing with the ball.

Talbot suspected something, bought the manuscript and the ball for a guinea, and as he had a friend, a Dr. John Dee, who was interested in hermetic science, he went to see him and showed him his find. Dee realised that the manuscript dealt with the philosopher's stone and with the methods of finding it, but that it did so in a symbolical form the meaning of which escaped him. He opened the white ball and found inside it a powder which was none other than the precious projection powder. With its help he was able at his first experiment in the presence of the astounded Talbot to make gold.

To describe Talbot as being astounded hardly conveys his condition. Most men lose their self-control under the influence of gold; for the royal metal with its dull glitter produces an intoxication which is more intense than that produced by any alcohol. It increases a man's base passions, his desire for physical gratification, avarice, vanity. Gripped by the lust for gold, Talbot made a pact with John Dee, whose help was indispensable to him for the operation of transmutation; and, as his reputation in England was exceedingly bad, a fact of which his cap reminded him at every turn, they began to travel.

The two companions, whose link was lust for gold, went to Bohemia and Germany. John Dee was still unable to understand the Catholic bishop's manuscript, but he could use the powder. The style they kept up and the lectures of Talbot, who boasted of being an adept and of being able to make gold at will, created a great stir wherever they went. The Emperor Maximilian II sent for Talbot and, with his entire court, was present at an attempt at transmutation. He immediately appointed Talbot Marshal of Bohemia. But what he wanted from him was not a small quantity of projection powder, but the secret of its production. He had Talbot watched and then imprisoned him so that the precious secret should not be lost. But Talbot was unable to reveal a secret he did not know, and the stock of the bishop's powder was nearly exhausted.

John Dee, who had been wise enough to realise his own ignorance and remain in obscurity, fled to England, where he sought and received the protection of Queen Elizabeth. The manuscript on which he had laboured seems to have kept its secret until his death, for he lived the last part of his life on a small pension given him by the queen. The arrogant Talbot killed one of his guards in an attempt to escape and died in his prison.

I have told this story to show that the secret of the philosopher's stone was not given to Nicolas Flamel alone, but that it was known from immemorial times, that it filtered through the ages by various means and was received by men in modern times, for their weal or woe, according to their capacity to understand and love their fellow beings.

History records many men who have been able to make gold. But this was only the first stage of the secret. The second gave the means of healing physical illnesses through the same agent which produced transmutation. To reach this stage a higher intelligence and a more complete disinterestedness were necessary. The third stage was accessible only to very few. Just as the molecules of metals are transformed under great increase of temperature, so the emotional elements in human nature undergo an increased intensity of vibrations which transforms them and makes them spiritual. In its third stage the secret of the philosopher's stone enabled a man's soul to attain unity with the divine spirit. The laws of Nature are alike for that which is above and for that which is below. Nature changes according to an ideal. Gold is the perfection of terrestrial substances, and it is to produce gold that minerals evolve. The human body is the model of the animal kingdom, and living forms orientate themselves in the direction of their ideal type. The emotional substance of the soul strives, through the filter of the senses, to transform itself into spirit and return to unity with the divine. The movements of Nature are governed by a single law, which is diverse in its manifestations but uniform in its essence. It was the discovery of this law that the alchemists sought. If there were many of them who discovered the mineral agent, fewer were able to find its application to the human body, and only a very few adepts knew of the essential agent, the sublime heat of the soul, which fuses the emotions, consumes the prison of form and allows entry into the higher world.

Raymond Lulle made gold for Edward III, King of England. George Ripley gave a hundred thousand pounds of alchemical gold to the Knights of Rhodes when they were attacked by the Turks. Gustavus Adolphus of Sweden had an enormous number of gold pieces coined which were marked with a special mark because they were of hermetic origin. They had been made by an unknown man under the protection of the king, who was found at his death to possess a considerable quantity of gold. In 1580 the Elector Augustus of Saxony, who was an alchemist, left a fortune of seventeen million rixdollars. The source of the fortune of Pope John XXII, whose residence was Avignon and whose revenues were small, must be ascribed to alchemy (at his death there were in his treasury twenty-five million florins). This must be concluded also in the case of the eighty-four quintals of gold possessed in 1680 by Rudolph II of Germany. The learned chemist Van Helmont and the doctor Helvetius, who were both of them sceptics with regard to the philosopher's stone and had even published books against it, were converted as a result of an identical adventure which befell them. An unknown man visited them and gave them a small quantity of projection powder; he asked them not to perform the transmutation until after his departure and then only with apparatus prepared by themselves, in order to avoid all possibility of fraud. The grain of powder given to Van Helmont was so minute that he smiled; the unknown man smiled also and took back half of it, saying that what was left was enough to make a large quantity of gold. Both Van Helmont's and Helvetius' experiments were successful, and both men became acknowledged believers in alchemy.*

Van Helmont was the greatest chemist of his day. If we do not hear nowadays that Madame Curie has had a mysterious visitor who gave her a little powder " the colour of the wild poppy and smelling of calcined sea salt," the reason may be that the secret is lost; or, possibly, now that alchemists are no longer persecuted or burnt, it may be that they no longer need the favourable judgment of those in official power.

Until the end of the eighteenth century it was customary to hang alchemists dressed in a grotesque gold robe on gilded gallows. If they escaped this punishment they were usually imprisoned by barons or kings, who either compelled them to make gold or extorted their secret from them in exchange for their liberty. Often they were left to starve in prison. Sometimes they were roasted by inches or had their limbs slowly broken. For when gold is the prize, religion and morality are effaced and human laws set at nought.

This is what happened to Alexander Sethon, called the Cosmopolitan. He had had the wisdom to hide all his life and avoid the company of the powerful. He was a truly wise man. However, he married. In order to please his wife, who was young and beautiful,

* Louis Figuier, *L'alchimie et les alchimistes.*

he yielded to the invitation extended him by the Elector of Saxony, Christian II, to come to his court. As he was unwilling to disclose the secret of the philosopher's stone, which he had long possessed, he was scalded every day with molten lead, beaten with rods and torn with needles till he died.

Michael Sendivogius, Botticher and Paykull spent part of their lives in prison, and many men suffered death for no other crime than the study of alchemy.

If a great number of these seekers were impelled by ambition, if there were among them charlatans and impostors, yet many of them cherished a genuine ideal of moral development. At all events their work in the domain of physics and chemistry formed a solid basis for the few wretched fragmentary scraps of knowledge which are called modern science, and are cause for great pride to a large number of ignorant men.

These men regard the alchemists as dreamers and fools, though every discovery of their infallible science is to be found in the dreams and follies of the alchemists. It is no longer a paradox, but a truth attested by recognised scientists themselves, that the few fragments of truth that we moderns possess are due to the pretended or genuine adepts who were hanged in the Middle Ages with a gilt dunce's cap on their heads.

Moreover, not all of them saw in the philosopher's stone the mere vulgar, useless aim of making gold. A small number of them received, either through a master or through the silence of daily meditation, higher truth.

These were the men who, by having observed it in themselves, understood the symbolism of the third essential rule of alchemy : *Use only one vessel, one fire and one instrument.*

They knew the characteristics of the sole agent, of the secret fire, of the serpentine power which moves upwards in spirals, " of the great primitive force hidden in all matter, organic and inorganic," which the Hindus call *kundalini*, which creates and destroys simultaneously. They calculated that the capacity for creation and the capacity for destruction were equal, that the possessor of the secret had power for evil as great as his power for good ; and just as nobody trusts a child with a high explosive, so they kept the divine science to themselves, or, if they left a written account of the facts they had found, they always omitted the essential point, so that it could be understood only by someone who already knew.

Examples of such men were, in the seventeenth century, Thomas Vaughan, called Philalethes, and, in the eighteenth century, Lascaris. It is possible to form some idea of the lofty thought of Philalethes from his book *Introitus ;* but Lascaris has left us nothing. Little is known of their lives. Both of them wandered about Europe teaching those whom they considered worthy of being taught. They made gold often, but only for special reasons. They did not seek glory, but shunned it. They had knowledge enough to foresee persecution and avoid it. They had neither fixed abode nor family. It is not known when and where they died.

It is probable that they attained the most highly developed state possible to man, that they accomplished the transmutation of their soul. While still living they

were members of the spiritual world. They had re-
generated their being, performed the task of man.
They were twice born. They devoted themselves to
helping their fellow-men ; this they did in the most
useful way, which does not consist in healing the ills
of the body or in improving men's physical state. They
used a higher method, which in the first instance can
be applied only to a small number, but eventually
affects all. They helped the noblest minds to reach
the goal which they had reached themselves. They
sought such men in the towns through which they passed,
and, generally, during their travels. They had no
school and no regular teaching, because their teaching
was on the border of the human and the divine. But
they knew that a word sown at a certain time in a certain
soul would bring results a thousand times greater than
those which could accrue from the knowledge gained
through books or ordinary science.

From the bottom of our hearts we ought to thank the
modest men who held in their hands the magical formula
which makes a man master of the world, a formula
which they took as much trouble to hide as they had
taken to discover it. For however dazzling and bright
the obverse of the medallion, its reverse is dark as night.
The way of good is the same as the way of evil, and
when a man has crossed the threshold of knowledge,
he has more intelligence but no more capacity for love.
He is even tempted to have less. For with knowledge
comes pride, and egoism is created by the desire to
uphold the development of qualities that he considers
sublime. Through egoism he returns to the evil which
he has tried to escape. Nature is full of traps, and the

higher he rises in the hierarchy of men, the more numerous and the better hidden are the traps.

Ascetics are fortunate in so far as their asceticism is in some measure obligatory, in so far as they have not the possibility ⁻of satisfying passions which are dormant in them and which they know only from having observed them in others. But how dramatic it would be if the door of their cell should suddenly open and disclose within reach of their hand all that they desire or might have desired! St Anthony in his desert was surrounded by nothing but dreams. He stretched out his arms to grasp them, and if he did not succumb to temptation it was only because the phantoms vanished when he sought to seize them. But the living, almost immediately tangible reality of gold, which gives every-thing—what superhuman strength would be necessary to resist it! That is what had to be weighed by the adepts who possessed the triple hermetic truth. They had to remember those of their number who had failed and fallen away so lightly. And they had to ponder how apparently illogical and sad for mankind is the law by which the tree of wisdom is guarded by a serpent infinitely more to be feared than the serpent which tempted Eve in the Garden of Eden.

CPSIA information can be obtained
at www.ICGtesting.com
Printed in the USA
BVHW03*0704241018
531086BV00011B/19/P